CONTENTS

INTRODUCTION

In this book we emphasise the importance of developing physical and pre-literacy skills as a precursor to reading and writing in the early years. Sometimes, expectations of very young children far exceed what they are really capable of in the way of formal activities. Children are being asked to use pencils and to form abstract symbols like letters before they have mastered gross motor skills like climbing, balancing and riding scooters and tricycles. If children are not exposed to adequate opportunities to develop their physical skills, they will not be able to perform the fine motor actions required to make progress in literacy. A significant number of children – boys in particular – need a generous amount of time to develop all the skills necessary for successful reading and writing. It would be a great shame if these children were unwittingly being set up to fail because adults' expectations were pitched at an inappropriate level.

While there are some useful guidelines outlining 'average' attainments, all children are unique and are ready for formal reading and writing at differing ages. (In many countries, children are not taught about reading and writing until the age of six or seven.) Hence, over-reliance upon developmental checklists can be misleading.

Staff in pre-schools can feel pressurised, however, by government targets and by parental expectations. It is valuable to help parents recognise that pre-schools are building up a wide range of skills in the early stages and are not exclusively focused on the formal teaching of reading skills. Some pre-schools provide workshops for parents and this is explored in further detail in Section 4 of this book.

Some children have specific difficulties with the whole business of reading, writing and spelling – others are early developers and talented in certain areas. Local education authorities (LEAs) have a policy and network of support for early years practitioners working with children who are exceptional in any way and the area Special Educational Needs Co-ordinators (SENCOs) can offer assistance. If children are beginning to read and write on entry to a pre-school setting, it is important to nurture their abilities and encourage their progress – but others will be far from ready to begin any sort of 'formal' learning. For these children, developing communication skills, motor co-ordination and visual and auditory discrimination will be of primary importance – alongside a love of stories and rhymes and a growing sense of self-esteem.

SECTION 1

Developing literacy skills

Communication development

Getting ready to read

Getting ready to write

Able children

Sensory processing

Developing thinking skills

Self-esteem and motivation

Special needs

Reading and writing are two skills that many people look at in relative isolation. It is generally expected that when a child starts school they will be taught to read and write. Some parents are understandably very proud and pleased when their pre-school child begins to develop these skills prior to starting school but it will be important that the child is developing a holistic approach to literacy development and learning. Reading and writing are both complex, high-level skills and all children benefit from sound preparation in 'getting ready' to read and write.

As a starting point we need to recognise that reading and writing are methods of communication. Reading is about gaining information and ideas from another person through decoding an abstract symbolic code. Writing is about sharing information with other people also through using an abstract symbolic code. It is essential to recognise that effective reading skills are about understanding the *meaning* behind a communication; good writing skills involve being able to express an idea or piece of information in words and being able to record in a way that other people can understand.

Communication development

Basic communication is the way that a message is passed on to another person. Before this communication can begin there are a range of steps that need to happen. First of all, the child needs to have good reasons to want to communicate and find out or give information. Motivation is absolutely vital for early communication and the later development of literacy skills and the focus in the early years should always be on this. If the child develops good verbal communication skills in a fun way, the likelihood is that reading and writing skills development will also be seen in a fun way.

According to Weitzman (1992) there are seven stages of communication and language development for normally developing children. These stages are outlined on the following page.

In order to be able to read and write a child will need to build up a large bank of words and be familiar with the way language is structured. It is very important therefore to encourage children's talking and listening skills. From the moment they make their first babbling noise and an adult responds, babies are beginning to learn how to communicate. Every opportunity should be taken to talk with pre-school children, especially those who – for whatever reason – are 'vulnerable' in terms of language development.

Early years practitioners should be aware of all the different ways to engage children in speaking and listening, and planning can include useful prompts. (See 'Water play – speaking and listening' (p. 4) for planning speaking opportunities around play with water.)

The seven stages of communication and language development

Adults respond to the child

The child may not communicate deliberately – but adults may respond as if the child is intending to communicate: responding to a gurgle as if it were a request.

Awareness and responding

The child shows awareness of other people and may pay attention to a person, or to a toy. Understanding of non-verbal cues begins and early understanding of some words, in familiar contexts. The child begins to respond to another person's communication. The child makes sounds, smiles and babbles.

Deliberate (non-verbal) communication begins

Now the child communicates deliberately – with intention. The child uses non-verbal communication at first: sounds, gestures, eye gaze, pointing. Joint attention begins to develop, as the child becomes able to share attention with both a person and a toy. The child uses (mostly non-verbal) communication for social purposes now and can take turns in a play situation. Jargon (strings of sounds that resemble words) may be heard and the child communicates primarily for social reasons and will persevere if not responded to.

First words and more understanding

Child uses a small number of words and understands them. The child's use of a word may be very broad or very narrow. Child communicates mainly for social reasons.

Joining words together

The child's understanding of words is developing and now words begin to be joined together. Vocabulary increases and the combinations of two words increase the range of messages that the child can express. The first questions are used, and verbal language can now be used to talk about the child's everyday activities, as they happen.

Longer sentences

The child's understanding and use of verbal language grows rapidly, as more and more words are joined together to form sentences – which now use more mature forms of grammar. The child begins to ask 'Why?' and can take part in conversation.

Conversation

Now the child understands more and more adult language and enjoys taking part in conversations. Ideas are joined together, by using words such as 'and': 'Mummy went to town and bought me a new jumper'. The child's vocabulary now includes several thousand words and verbal language is used to think, learn and imagine.

(*Source:* from Weitzman, E. (1992) *Learning, Language and Loving It*)

Water play – speaking and listening

Vocabulary: big, small (bigger, smaller), wet, dry, heavy (heavier), full, empty, pour, flow, sink, float, warm, cool, cold (warmer, colder), splash, waves, deep, shallow, (plus equipment names)

Questions

- Can you find something that you think will float/sink?

- How shall we keep our clothes dry?

- How many cups of water will we need to fill this jug?

- What will happen if we put this stone into the jug (which is full of water)?

- Which cup is the heavier? (one full of water, one half empty)

- What will happen if we put a sponge into the water?

- This cup floats, but what will happen if we fill it with water?

- Who has been in the water at the paddling pool/swimming pool/seaside – was it warm or cold?

- What sort of creatures live in/on the water?

- Who knows some ways of getting across the water in a river or a pond?

- **Comment** on what the children are doing – give them the language to give back to you:
  Adult: 'I can see that you like painting, Kerry. Those flowers look like daisies in a lovely green field.'
  Child: 'Yes . . . daisies in lovely green field.'
- **Ask questions**, both 'open' and 'closed'. A closed question is where there is a right or wrong answer: 'Amjit, how many ducks can you see in the water?' Young children can often cope with this sort of question quite well. Open questions can have several appropriate answers: 'Lily, what do you like to eat for your tea?' Children can find this sort of question very difficult and the adult may need to offer support by reducing the number of answers possible: 'Matthew, what do you like best for tea? – jacket potato or pasta?'

  By saying the child's name first – before the question – you are alerting them to be listening and paying attention and increasing their chances of being able to respond. Get into the habit of giving children time to think before they answer (perhaps count to five); sometimes it is tempting to jump in and answer for them – but this is not always necessary if you can give them a little time to think.

  Build up a repertoire of responses to wrong and inappropriate or irrelevant answers and avoid saying 'No', or, 'That isn't quite right,' or, 'That's wrong.' Negative responses can damage a child's self-esteem and discourage them from volunteering answers next time. (See below for some suggested responses to inappropriate answers.)

Responding to inappropriate answers

That's an interesting idea . . .

Hmmmm . . . I can see how you're thinking . . . who else has got an idea? (When other children have answered appropriately, return to the first child and ask, 'James, what do you think now?')

That's nearly right . . . Well done for having a go.

I like that answer – let's see if anyone else has got an idea.

I see what you mean . . .

Let's come back to that later . . . For now, I really want to think about . . .

Thank you for telling us about that . . . Can we come back to (the subject in hand) now . . .

I would love to hear about . . . another time/later/after play . . . just now we are all thinking about . . .

That's an interesting answer and it shows good thinking . . . have you remembered . . .

You're trying very hard . . . well done.

- **Model** good language structures. There is a subtle but effective way of doing this without seeming to correct the child.

  Adult: 'Suzi, what have you got in your café for me to eat today?'

  Child: 'Me got cake.'

  Adult: 'Oh good! *I've* got some cakes at home, but can I have one of yours to eat now, please?'

Getting ready to read

Most children learn to read – in their own good time – without too much difficulty. For some, however, the process can be much harder, often because the 'pre-reading' skills are not well established. There are lots of ways to prepare children for learning to read and many teachers believe that more time needs to be spent on these areas.

Language experience

This has been touched on above – the better a child can speak, the more words he or she knows and the better they can understand others, the more prepared they will be for reading. It is important to remember however, that books are not always written in the same way as we speak. *'W'im goo-in t'the chippie'* will be a familiar phrase used by families in the Midlands, but in a story book may well appear as 'We're going to the chip shop.' Children who hear stories read to them from an early age can understand these differences and learn to take them in their stride.

Phonological awareness

Learning about letter sounds (phonics) and being able to put them together to build words, is an important part of both reading and writing. To be able to do this, children have to be able to hear sounds clearly and differentiate between similar sounds. The incidence of 'glue' ear or other problems, can seriously affect a child's ability in this area. In the early years, games to practise sound differentiation can be great fun, and repeating rhymes also provides valuable experience in phonological awareness. For example:

  Humpty Dumpty sat on a *wall*

  Humpty Dumpty had a great _____ (Let children provide the rhyming word, point out that 'fall' rhymes with 'wall' – they sound alike.)

Check that children can:
- hear that two or more words begin with the same sound
- identify the odd one out
- pick out two words that rhyme

Understanding books

Children need to know that the print in a book conveys meaning. The pictures can give us clues about a story – but the words are where we look to get most information. They also need to know:

- about holding the book the right way up
- how to turn pages – one at a time
- where to start reading – left to right along the line – and about the 'return sweep' to the next line and that the story goes from front to back (usually)
- that one word on the page matches one word spoken

This knowledge comes from sharing books with adults, following the finger-pointing as the reader moves along the line of text (progressing to the child pointing at the words) and being involved in the whole process rather than being passive.

Visual discrimination and memory

Children have to be able to see the difference between similar-looking squiggles on the page and remember which sounds they represent: p looks very much like q, b like d, m like n. Before practitioners embark on letter–sound recognition, activities to develop visual discrimination (sorting, matching, spot the difference, find the odd one out etc.) can provide useful practice in this skill. Kim's game and other visual memory activities are also useful. There are many words in the English language which have to be remembered from the way they look rather than from their individual letter sounds – *the*, *why*, *could* – so visual memory plays an important part in learning to read.

Prediction

Early readers need to be able to have a good guess at what a word might be, using all the clues available:

- Look at the picture
- Look at the first letter – what sound does it make?
- Think about what sort of word would fit there
- Think about what makes sense

If a child has a good experience of the world and a good vocabulary, he or she will guess the last word of this sentence:

It was raining so Kim put up her umbrella.

There might be a picture to check against – and if he or she knows the sound made by the first letter, the child can be pretty sure that the word is 'umbrella' even if they have never seen it before.

Context

Early readers will be most comfortable with stories set in familiar contexts and introducing the book to them before reading begins, will help to establish the context and explain any new vocabulary. Even before children have begun to read for themselves, looking at the cover of the book and the pictures inside can help to 'set the scene' and 'cue in' the audience for what they can expect to happen.

- Talk about key aspects of pictures drawing attention to main characters or objects
- Ask questions about what might happen next. Involve the child in thinking ahead
- Was the child right in what they thought?
- Keep checking to ensure the child is able to understand

Getting ready to write

The developmental pre-writing stages that children seem to go through include:
- making random scribble patterns
- arranging scribbles in lines
- making squiggles and letter-like shapes which may include a few real letter shapes
- using letters to represent one or more sounds, e.g. S for Samantha
- some complete words appear

During these stages, children are learning how to hold and control a pencil or crayon and those with motor co-ordination difficulties will benefit from support in choosing an appropriate size and thickness of pencil, using the right amount of pressure and practising an appropriate pencil grip. Children who are left handed have particular issues to manage and practitioners need to know strategies to show them. (See *Handwriting* by Taylor (2001) – details are provided in 'Further reading'.)

Most children will want to copy adults and will attempt to 'write' letters and cards. Encouraging this is very important because by doing this they are learning about sending messages and communicating. Adults in the early years setting should model writing in a variety of situations and the setting up of a post office or writing corner/table can provide lots of opportunity for this.

Able children

There will be those children who show a particular interest in the world around them and present as very able children. There is now a greater interest and awareness of the needs of highly able children and their entitlement to have their needs addressed. These children can often be recognised by the following characteristics. They:

- are highly curious
- master core skills easily
- ask challenging questions
- have unusual ideas
- can be intense and persistent
- can transfer skills easily to other areas
- are often avid readers
- are often beyond the group
- have good memories

It is recognised that there is no single best way to support these children and that early years advisers can often provide advice on how to most effectively develop the child's interests. As with all children the most important place to start is with the child's own interests. Local libraries can provide a range of books. These children can be encouraged to develop their own topic books and may benefit by being encouraged to share their ideas with groups of children. It will be essential that the social and emotional aspects continue to be developed. If children show a particular aptitude for reading they could be encouraged through the paired or reciprocal reading approaches.

The most helpful way to support these children is through enriching the skills they already have. Some suggestions might be:

- the child having their own resource box or folder which can be added to over time. This could include puzzles, word searches, crosswords, games and pictures
- encouraging the child to make their own books on subjects they are interested in
- facilities for the child to make up their own stories and act them out through puppets
- art and craft materials to make their own cards, puppets etc.
- a child's daily diary either in pictures or words
- a tape recorder to record the child's stories
- a specific daily fun task for the child which could be in the box when the child arrives, e.g. a word search or data collecting task
- looking for information in a book (see Further Reading (p. 88) for suggested texts).

Sensory processing

Another very important area for reading and writing readiness is connected to bodily awareness and integration of all the information that is being presented to children. At any one time there are several senses that are being stimulated and children need to have effective mechanisms for integrating these. They need to be able to recognise the important information and what needs to be screened out. They also need to be able to link the different senses together. It can be very difficult for children to do this if there is a very lively, stimulating environment and they are not clear which aspect to prioritise.

For example when learning new vocabulary the child needs to clearly hear the word spoken, they need to see the object it refers to and they often need to touch the object so they are familiar with it and then repeat the word. If there is background television noise and other noisy children around, the child may be unable to screen out the background noises.

Sensory integration is a term you may have come across, particularly with regard to children with motor skill difficulties. These children have difficulty with learning because their brains are not processing the information they receive through the senses of:

- touch
- sight
- sound
- taste
- smell

Children with a range of learning difficulties often exhibit a slow or confused sensory processing system and need very simple chunks of information in order to make sense of this information.

Sensory development is considered the foundation block of future learning. If there is not enough sensory-based information it is extremely difficult to move on to developing sensory integration abilities or form concepts or relationships between objects. This will impact on all future learning including reading and writing skills which depend on using a multisensory approach for effective learning.

Children who have difficulty with processing information may:

- cry continuously when they are not being held or insist that particular people hold them
- always topple or become unsteady when they are trying to sit, stand or use steps
- have a tremor when sitting without firm support
- have slower saving reactions
- be heavy footed or heavy handed
- constantly seek out semi-resistant materials or objects to squeeze, pinch, bite or chew
- be unaware of bumps and bruises and have a high pain threshold
- love rough and tumble to the point of being in danger or creating dangerous situations and have no awareness of this
- often be quite rough without being aware of the effect this has on others – they may be seen as destructive or spiteful

These difficulties all impact specifically on writing skills where there needs to be a high level of physical co-ordination and organisation of thoughts.

There are also children who find it difficult to process bodily awareness through gravity and motion. This will impact on motor skills development, sequencing and self-esteem, all of which affect reading and writing skills. These children may:

- avoid movement
- cling on tightly when being carried or moved
- intensely dislike moving backwards or lying back unless the movements are very slow, deliberate and predictable
- avoid exploring their environment beyond the immediate proximity
- dislike new environments
- be late to sit up, kneel or walk
- display heightened and therefore poorly planned saving reactions
- avoid or become anxious when using steps and stairs
- avoid play equipment that takes them off of their centre of balance
- avoid or become anxious in the company of other children

It will be important to be aware of the needs of these children and not pressurise them into activities for which they are not ready. These children are still making sense of their environment through a slower processing of information and will need to develop confidence. It may be that some of these children will need more specialised help in developing these skills. If there are continued concerns the above points or the 'Checklists for identifying a child with dyspraxia' in Appendix 1 may provide useful information to professionals such as an occupational therapist.

Developing thinking skills

In recent years there has been increasing importance attributed to thinking skills and teaching these skills is playing an ever-increasing role in the learning curriculum. The main reason for this is that learning requires active participation by learners and includes the process of reflecting on the information received. A crucial aspect of early years education is to promote effective thinking in young children. In order to do this, early years educators will need to become familiar with specific techniques for developing these skills and there are now also a number of programmes available for younger learners (see Further Reading, p.88).

One particular programme which has been tried and tested in a number of early years settings is the six Thinking Hats devised by Edward de Bono. This and other methods are explained in more detail in *Teach Your Child How to Think* (de Bono 1992). Although Edward de Bono recommends this method for older children it has been successfully adapted in several early years settings.

This method focuses on six distinct thinking styles, associating each style of thinking with a specific colour. Six coloured hats can be made or bought for this. The idea is to wear one hat at a time and to really focus on developing different styles of thinking. Each hat has a different job to do:

- White – the information hat. What do we know already? It helps children to recognise what is the actual evidence.
- Red – the feelings hat. How do I feel? How does Sam feel?
- Black – this hat is used for any wariness or criticisms of the subject being discussed. What do you think could be stopping us?
- Yellow – this hat is about the good things about the subject. What are all the good things about this?
- Green – the hat for new ideas. What can we do?
- Blue – this hat is for thinking about where we are now and thinking about the next step. What do we need to do now?

There is no right or wrong way to use the hats but it is best to introduce them one at a time so that the children become familiar with each thinking style. The hats can be used systematically in a sequence or you can focus on one or two hats only during a session. The system can be very easy to teach to young children and they can become involved in a wide range of problem-solving activities in the pre-school setting. The hats can be used with small or big groups so that more children have the opportunity to express their ideas. The adult can either direct the order in which the hats are presented or can ask for ideas and then check which hat was used. Eventually, children will be able to use the ideas without the hat props being there.

How the hats were used in one pre-school

Martin (aged three years) had been admitted to hospital. He had only recently started at pre-school and his mother had sent in a message to say that he would be in hospital as he had problems with his breathing. A group of six children were engaged in an exercise about what they could do. They used the six thinking hats, led by an adult.

- White Hat: Martin is in hospital with breathing problems. We want him to know that we are thinking about him.
- Red Hat: It makes me feel very sad because Martin can't play with the sand and he won't be able to join in our sports day. Martin must be very upset.
- Green Hat: We could make him a card and all of us can draw him a picture of us all at sports day and then Martin will know we are thinking about him. We could take him a present.
- Yellow Hat: Yes, that would be good. We can find out his address and go and visit him. He will know that we are still thinking about him.
- Black Hat: We'd best ask his mum first. We could ask his mum what sort of present he would like before we get it. We need to collect some money as well or else we'll have to make him something from the things we have here or make a present at home and take it to him.
- Blue Hat: So, we can make him a card and someone can take it to his house. We can then ask what sort of present he would like.

Self-esteem and motivation

In any learning situation it is always best to start with the child's interest and experience. Adults can help children by sharing in the child's developing skills and praising children for effort. In this way children will develop a high level of self-esteem and be willing to attempt the more difficult aspects of literacy skills which will eventually follow. Any observation will quickly show which activities or areas a child shows interest in. Some suggestions are:

- A useful starting point with reading can be to use photographs of the child doing things they enjoy and making a very repetitive book such as an 'I like . . .' book or an 'I can . . .' book. In this way the child has got cues from the pictures and all children will be proud of their reading achievements. This book can be shared with other family members, friends and pre-school staff. The next step could be matching the words and then encouraging the child to make their own sentence.

- A similar book can be made using pictures of toys from catalogues, food packets etc. and making a highly repetitive 'I like . . .' book.

- Children can be encouraged to make their own interest books, cutting out pictures from catalogues etc. They can talk about the pictures and how they collected them.

- A large group book can be fun to make where children draw or cut out pictures or even make up a story.

- Paired reading provides a relatively stress-free way of starting reading (see 'Paired reading' in Section 4).

- Picture sequencing activities can provide language experiences where children try to tell the story from the pictures. This encourages children to look at relevant aspects of pictures and how the story develops sequentially. The children need to be encouraged to discuss the pictures and why they are selecting that particular order.

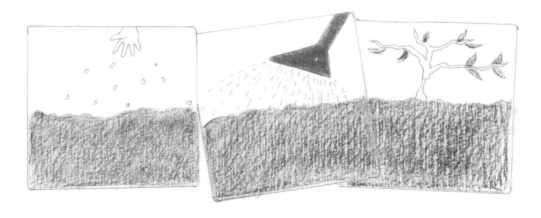

Special needs

Learning to read and write demands a wide variety of skills in children with a normal development pattern. Children with special educational needs will require additional awareness and support. The area Special Educational Needs Co-ordinator (SENCO) will be able to advise on specific issues and/or contact other professionals such as a speech and language therapist, occupational therapist and educational psychologist. There are contact details given in 'Useful addresses' at the back of this book for organisations providing support and information.

The following are a range of children's difficulties that are likely to need additional support.

Attention Deficit Hyperactivity Disorder (ADHD)

Children with ADHD have difficulties with perseverance, may be easily distracted, have short-term memory and poor organisation skills. They may find it very difficult to sit still and stay on task.

What can help?

- Give very short tasks with a reward on completion
- Try to minimise distractions. Some children benefit by being in a quiet area
- Always praise for effort
- Use visual clues. Give very simple instructions to the child. When giving verbal instructions ask the child to picture the activity in their head or take a mental 'photo' of what you will be doing, e.g. I want you to sit in the book corner. Ask the child about the 'photo'. What are they doing? What are they sitting on? Where possible, use a visual or concrete clue
- Find out what the child enjoys most and use this to motivate them

Autistic Spectrum Disorder (ASD or autism)

These children have difficulties with social interaction, communication and using their imagination. They may have difficulty in understanding stories outside their own experience and can get upset over changes in routine.

What can help?

- Always be clear about what you expect the child to do, e.g. I want you to choose three different colours and colour in the picture of the flower
- Use visual cues where possible. Show the child what you want
- Use a visual timetable so that the child knows that the activity will change in five minutes (you could use a sand timer or egg timer to illustrate this)
- Some children benefit by being in a quiet corner away from noisy activities and brightly coloured displays
- Always refer to the child by name

Cerebral Palsy

Children with cerebral palsy have difficulties with motor control, are frustrated at not being able to physically achieve their aims and have a reduced level of achievement.

What can help?
- Always praise for effort
- Tell the child you know this must be frustrating for them and that you recognise they are doing their best
- Use an adult or another child to carry out the activity on occasions with the child giving verbal instructions if possible
- Refer to a physiotherapist or occupational therapist for advice (there will often be a multidisciplinary team involved with the child – make contact as soon as possible and find out about any care plan that has been put in place)
- Allow more time for activities
- If the child uses a mobility aid, ensure there is enough space in the setting for easy access
- Be sensitive about toileting arrangements
- Help other children to accept that the child is different, and understand how to help them

Dyslexia

Children with dyslexia have difficulties with sequencing, word recognition, organisation, short-term memory, self-esteem.

What can help?
- Give visual instructions one at a time and check for understanding
- Send the child on errands and messages to help to develop their short-term memory
- Games such as matching pairs and Kim's game may be useful
- Praise for effort
- Develop phonological awareness by singing/saying lots of songs and rhymes
- Provide help with developing organisational skills – collecting equipment, dressing for outdoor play etc.

Dyspraxia (or Developmental Co-ordination Disorder – DCD)

Children with dyspraxia have difficulties with motor skill development, co-ordination, organisation, sequencing, self-esteem and hand–eye co-ordination.

What can help?
- Praise for effort
- Use a marker so that the child knows where to start writing or drawing

- Have all equipment ready, explore different writing tools, pencil grips etc.
- Implement a motor skill programme (preferably designed by an occupational therapist)
- Use pre-writing activities for teaching left to right movements
- Use tracing activities
- Be aware that the child may tire easily because they have to make so much effort

Hearing impairment and 'glue' ear (intermittent hearing)

Children with a hearing impairment have difficulties with hearing sounds correctly, they may 'switch off' because they are not hearing what is said, may suffer from anxiety and have problems with balance.

What can help?
- Ensure the child has eye contact when you talk to them and check their understanding
- Use taped story books where the child can use headphones to follow the story
- Use gestures and visual prompts as back-up
- Check with parents that appropriate hearing assessments have been made
- Consider whether an induction loop would help

Speech and language difficulties

Children with speech and language difficulties have problems with making speech sounds and/or putting thoughts into words. There may also be receptive language difficulties – understanding what others say – and what is written down.

What can help?
- Keep language simple and clear
- Praise for effort
- Give instructions one at a time to ensure that the child understands what is expected
- Use visual clues
- Check to ensure that the child understands stories and information
- Model language
- Match comments to the child's attempts
- Use proper names
- Speak to the child on their own level to ensure maximum eye contact
- Expand the child's message
- Use choices
- Use questions carefully – according to the child's ability to understand and respond – and allow time for answers

SECTION 2

Case studies

Children

1. A child with little or no eye contact
2. A child who makes no sound at all
3. A child who has no verbal speech
4. A child with a poor speech sound system
5. A child who fidgets during story time
6. A child who has very poor co-ordination
7. A child who has poor attention and listening skills
8. A child with limited vocabulary
9. A child who shows no interest in story time
10. A child who has difficulty with balance
11. A child with dexterity problems
12. A child with poor visual tracking
13. A child who cannot remember nursery rhymes and who presents with a generalised delay in the acquisition of speech
14. A child who does not recognise facial gestures
15. A child who appears distractible and presents with disruptive behaviours
16. A child who is inconsistent in levels of achievement and who gives up easily

Practice

17. A session on letter sounds
18. Story time
19. Writing your name
20. Recognising and writing letter sounds
21. Making a Mother's Day card
22. Reading to a small group

CASE STUDY 1

A child with little or no eye contact

Natalie enjoys sitting at the table and drawing. She will settle happily at a puzzle table and work through all the puzzles on the table. She enjoys outdoor play and follows the other children out when they go out. Staff are concerned that she does not look at them when they speak to her. She will sometimes answer with a 'yes' or a 'no' indicating that she does understand. Staff have tried to engage her in a conversation but she is reluctant to say anything and looks away.

Possible reasons for this behaviour

Natalie may:
- have hearing difficulties
- have a difficulty with processing language. She can answer simple questions with a 'yes' or a 'no' but may have difficulties in responding to open-ended questions or being asked her viewpoint
- have a cultural background that does not encourage children to look directly at adults
- have social communication difficulties
- find it difficult to look at someone and listen to what they are saying at the same time

Strategies

- Natalie will need to develop conversation skills and the ability to respond to questions. It would be most helpful to focus on these skills and not on the eye contact. If pressure is taken off eye contact, Natalie may feel more confident in responding
- Natalie may need opportunities to make choices. Initially this could be a choice between something she really wants and something that does not concern her, such as the choice between a puzzle and a plastic plate. Natalie would be shown both and asked to choose
- Puppets and miniature toys could be used to develop conversation skills in a fun way. Natalie could be shown how to make choices through this
- Natalie could be helped by looking at books with an adult with a small group of children. Initially the pictures would be looked at and the children encouraged to say what is in each picture. Gradually more open single questions would be asked, e.g. 'What is the cat doing?'

CASE STUDY 2

A child who makes no sound at all

Jasmin has never spoken to anyone at pre-school. She plays with a range of equipment on her own but does not relate to other children. She looks very uneasy and sullen when adults are talking to her. The other pre-school children 'look after' her and often talk for her, especially at registration or if anybody asks her a question. This is particularly so if anybody comes into the pre-school. Some of the children will say, 'Jasmin never talks.'

Possible reasons for this behaviour

Jasmin:
- has elected not to speak at pre-school
- has difficulties understanding what is said to her
- is very conscious about mixing with people in the pre-school
- may be the youngest in her family and enjoys all the positive aspects of being the youngest, such as not speaking

Strategies

Check whether Jasmin talks at home. In many of these situations, the children are reported to talk happily at home. If so, a family member could come along to pre-school so that Jasmin can become accustomed to talking here too. Gradually, another child could be added to this family group. (It can be helpful to record discussions with parents/carers – see 'Meeting with parents/carers' form in Appendix 2.)

There are a number of children who exhibit elective mutism where they choose not to speak in a specific setting. Almost all children will outgrow this fairly quickly but it can last up to about nine years of age. If elective mutism is suspected it is advisable not to put pressure on Jasmin to speak. She should be encouraged to make acknowledgements non-verbally, e.g. with a nod of the head or grunt, and other children should be encouraged not to speak for Jasmin.

The reasons for elective mutism vary but for some children withholding speech can be very controlling and these children will need to recognise that they are still expected to join in with group activities. In these activities it will be important that Jasmin does not develop habits of becoming dependent on others.

A worrying aspect for adults can be their concern that the child will not learn until they speak. Research does not support this and most children develop normally in cognitive areas.

Some children can develop a 'learned helplessness' where they expect that others will do things for them. This can result in feelings of inadequacy and low self-esteem in the child. This will significantly impact on the child's approach to future learning including reading and writing. This reluctance to speak could have a significant impact on the child's ability to form concepts using language. It will be important that adults are aware of this and encourage participation in all activities.

In cases where the child does not speak, stories can be read to the child and the child can be asked to point out words or point to details in pictures. Pressure should not be put on a child to speak.

CASE STUDY 3

A child who has no verbal speech

Damien started pre-school at two years of age as he had not developed any speech. Although he has now been at pre-school for nine months he still does not have any clear words. He can use interaction and babble and lead an adult by the hand if he wants something.

Possible reasons for this behaviour

Damien may have:
- significant learning difficulties
- difficulties in developing language skills
- social communication difficulties which impact on his language, communication and interaction
- not had very much stimulation or opportunities to develop his skills as a result of a difficult early upbringing

Strategies

- It will be important to monitor Damien's rate of progress in specific non-verbal areas such as matching, sorting, puzzles. A very slow rate of development in these areas, in addition to his language difficulties, could indicate more generalised learning difficulties
- Damien may benefit from a speech and language assessment so that a programme can be put into place both at pre-school and at home
- Damien will need to be monitored in such areas as social interaction, play and communication so that information can be provided to other professionals should his difficulties continue
- Damien would benefit by having a carefully targeted individual education programme (IEP) in place so that his rate of learning can be identified. He may need programmes that rely on a very high level of repetition
- It would be helpful to discuss Damien's difficulties and specific areas for development with his parents or carers so that similar activities can be carried out at home
- Damien may need a much higher level of support with pre-reading and pre-writing skills, than his peers. At this stage he will need support with basic vocabulary. A starting point could be by asking Damien, 'Where's the car?' and giving him two objects – a car and another object (e.g. cup) – to choose from
- Damien may benefit from using a Picture Exchange Communication System (PECS) where he shows a picture of the object or activity he wants. For example he could show a picture of a cup when he wants a drink

CASE STUDY 4

A child with a poor speech sound system

Kieran has always been a happy boy at pre-school. He plays happily with all the boys and smiles at children and adults as they approach him. Pre-school staff have noticed that recently Kieran has been moving away when children start to talk to him. Kieran has had difficulties with many of his sounds and it is very difficult to work out what he is saying. A member of staff had observed one of the older children had told Kieran, 'You're really funny when you talk. It sounds like a baby.'

Possible reasons for this behaviour

Kieran may:
- have verbal dyspraxia where he has weakened speech muscles and cannot make accurate sounds
- be generally delayed in his speech communication
- be frightened to talk to people in case they laugh at him and consequently he is not able to develop his speech
- enjoy the positive aspects of being younger and he may not have developed his speech as he wishes to be thought of as being younger
- have learning difficulties

Strategies

- Kieran would benefit from a speech and language therapy assessment to determine the extent of his difficulties and to offer a programme of support
- Kieran may need to use a supportive communication system such as PECS or signing system. In some cases a child is more likely to develop speech sounds when the pressure is taken away from speech sounds
- It would be useful to discuss concerns with parents or carers and find out how Kieran communicates at home and also his position in the family
- It will be important that children in the pre-school are told that Kieran has difficulties so that they can encourage him to answer with concrete or visual cues
- Kieran will need a hearing test to ensure he is hearing sounds correctly. Hearing difficulties can have a significant impact on a child's speech and future development of building up phonic skills, which they will need to use in their reading and writing

CASE STUDY 5

A child who fidgets during story time

Jangheer rushes in to pre-school and runs around the outside of the hall. He waits until all the big toys are put out and always rushes to the sit-on toys. He will push other children off the toys. Jangheer usually plays quite happily if led to activities by an adult and shown what to do. He has significant difficulties when asked to sit in a small group at circle time. He constantly fidgets and bottom shuffles, knocking into other children as he does so. Even when seated on an adult's lap he will fidget and fiddles with the adult's hair and buttons.

Possible reasons for this behaviour

Jangheer may:
- have difficulties in focusing on activities. He may not have had any experience of settling down at an activity where he is not specifically engaged. There may also be indications of attention deficit hyperactivity disorder (ADHD)
- live in a household where he has not experienced books
- have limited understanding of language and of how to follow a story

Strategies

- It will be important to check out Jangheer's understanding of verbal language
- Jangheer may benefit from group activities which are initially more interactive and which involve movement, such as action rhymes and songs, or games, such as musical chairs or using musical instruments
- Jangheer may benefit from the well-defined structure of each session at pre-school so that he becomes aware of an order of activities. A visual programme may help so that Jangheer has clear expectations. It will be important that Jangheer understands what the pictures in the visual programme mean. The first picture or photograph on the programme could be of a bike/sit-on toy indicating the first activity as Jangheer comes in. The next picture could be of a sand or water tray. In this way Jangheer will become aware of the sequence of activities. This is a very important pre-literacy skill
- To assist Jangheer in becoming familiar with books and how to follow a story he could be encouraged to look at fun books, such as pop-up books or books with sounds and textures. This could be done on an individual basis or working in a small group. It is important that he recognises that books can be fun

CASE STUDY 6

A child who has very poor co-ordination

Billy's mum described him as having 'two left feet'. He constantly trips over as he makes his way around the pre-school. Billy's mum says that shopping is a 'nightmare' with Billy as he constantly trips over or bumps into things and knocks over displays. Billy cannot yet manage a spoon and usually resorts to eating with his fingers. At pre-school Billy has a very heavy-handed approach to puzzles as he tries to force pieces into a slot on the puzzle. He holds a paintbrush and wax crayons in a very tight grip and has a very heavy touch. When he puts the brush into the paint pot the paint often splashes outside of the pot and sometimes the pot gets knocked over.

Possible reasons for this behaviour

Billy may:
- be developing co-ordination skills at a slower rate than other children
- not have had the practice or the encouragement required to successfully manipulate small movements
- be used to eating with his fingers at home – or being fed – so using a spoon at mealtimes needs further practice
- have dyspraxic difficulties or sensory integration problems

Strategies

- Encourage Billy to slow down his movements and practise being more precise in his movements. He may need to be shown how to do this
- Help him to build towers of bricks, initially using large sponge blocks and gradually building up to larger wooden bricks. In this way he will learn to control his movements and relax his grip
- Show him some finger and hand exercises (see 'Finger fun activities' in Section 3) so that he begins to recognise when his movements are more relaxed. If Billy continues holding pencils with a tight grip it will make it very difficult for him when he begins to make letter shapes

If Billy does not respond to these interventions, it would be useful to make arrangements for an assessment by a paediatrician or occupational therapist so that a specific programme can be put into place.

CASE STUDY 7

A child who has poor attention and listening skills

Joshua happily plays with the trains and cars (chattering to himself) and will join in any activities that he is led to. He particularly likes the playdough and sand and water trays and will constantly chatter. He finds it very hard to sit on the carpet at registration time and even when his name is called out he does not respond. Often another child will answer for him. Although Joshua will sit in a circle for group sessions he is constantly looking around and sometimes rolling about. He often smiles at other children and sometimes starts to talk to them. Joshua's mum laughs and says she needs to repeat everything several times to Joshua.

Possible reasons for this behaviour

Joshua may:
- have hearing difficulties
- be 'talking in his head' as he is almost constantly chattering the rest of the time and he may be oblivious of the other sounds going on
- not be fully aware that he needs to respond
- be aware that others will answer for him or will repeat what is said. There is no real need for him to listen

Strategies

- Joshua would benefit from a hearing assessment to eliminate any difficulties in this area
- Joshua will need to be taught specific listening skills. Initially he may need to be taught to respond to anyone saying his name. There will need to be a specific programme in place for this, e.g. Joshua will receive a smiley face sticker when he responds to his name. If he gets four stickers he would then have a special reward which has been agreed with him
- Joshua would benefit from games to encourage attention and listening. There is a wide range available which include animal noises, lotto and games such as 'Guess who?' which encourages attention to detail
- Joshua could be given a special responsibility for taking simple messages so that he has to listen carefully to the instructions. He will need to be rewarded for this
- Attention and listening are very important pre-literacy skills as early reading and writing are developed on good skills in these areas. This is in visual and auditory areas. Joshua will need to learn to listen and work carefully so that he is using both senses effectively. Reading and writing are both skills that require a multisensory approach

CASE STUDY 8

A child with limited vocabulary

Leo is three and a half years old but still uses mainly gesture to make his needs known. He points to items he wants to play with and to things he would like to eat at snack time. When his key worker plays with him and asks him what he would like to play with he will use some single words like 'car' and 'bike'. In other situations, when using equipment like beads and small domestic and farm animals for matching and sorting or sequencing activities, Leo seems to have no idea what they are called. During one-to-one story sessions, Leo appears not to focus on the picture books and doesn't respond when asked to find something in the illustrations.

Possible reasons for this behaviour

Leo may have:
- a hearing and/or a visual problem
- had very limited experiences outside the pre-school
- a limited vocabulary indicative of generalised learning difficulties
- very limited receptive language skills
- had very little concrete or direct experience of the world
- had little or no experience of books and so may not be used to focusing on abstract visual stimuli

Strategies

- Referral to a paediatrician would help to eliminate any possible medical reason for this behaviour
- Referral to a speech and language therapist would help to clarify reasons and give some strategies for teaching
- Give Leo lots of direct physical experiences, e.g. gross motor activities, climbing, balancing, riding scooters and tricycles, making large arm movements which cross the midline of the body, making shapes in sand with his fingers etc.
- Staff should concentrate on encouraging Leo to name body parts, objects in his bedroom, his toys, his clothes, his house, his garden and then things in the pre-school
- Use rhyme to help Leo get into a rhythm with speech
- Use a visually strong method of teaching
- Use repetition to consolidate learning
- If Leo is not ready to start formal reading and writing skills in spite of his age, staff should teach him according to his developmental level and provide as many multisensory opportunities as possible

CASE STUDY 9

A child who shows no interest in story time

Lyndsay tends to flit from one activity to another in the pre-school. Generally, she will co-operate with adult requests and seems to enjoy being in the setting and playing with the other children. However, during whole-group story times, Lyndsay finds sitting on the carpet very difficult and often gets up and wanders off to play with toys in the room. When this happens, adults physically intervene and attempt to put Lyndsay back where she was sitting. This sets up a confrontation which is becoming disruptive.

Possible reasons for this behaviour

Lyndsay:
- has poor receptive language skills and does not understand the story and therefore loses any interest in it
- finds the group too big and this makes it impossible for her to concentrate in this situation
- has poor attention and listening skills (may have a hearing problem)

Strategies

- Consider having smaller groups for story time
- Let Lyndsay share a book with an adult initially on her own. If this is successful an adult could sit next to Lyndsay during group story time, holding a copy of the book that is being read (see an example of an IEP developed for Lyndsay in Appendix 2)
- Use puppets – these might promote interest
- Use rhyme and songs with actions to engage all the children
- Ask the children to look out for certain things in the story
- Use giant sized books so that children can see the pictures easily
- Keep story times short at first

CASE STUDY 10

A child who has difficulty with balance

Alice falls over all the time even when she is just walking from one activity to another in the pre-school. She has difficulty negotiating steps and avoiding equipment around the room. Alice has become very conscious of this and seems hesitant whenever she has to do anything physical. She is behind her peers with fine motor skills and cannot trace over giant shapes with a large pencil. This is causing concern because she is due to start school shortly.

Possible reasons for this behaviour

Alice may:
- be so worried about falling that all her concentration is on this, consequently affecting development in other areas
- have missed out on vital early physical development and this is now affecting her progress with more formal skills like writing
- have developed later than many other children, or there may be a genetic reason for Alice's clumsiness
- not have experienced much physical activity

Strategies

- Alice should avoid too much sitting and watching TV
- Advise Alice's parents/carers to let her walk to school as much as possible
- Old fashioned games like hopscotch and country dancing might help with co-ordination skills
- Traditional gym activities may help with improving body awareness
- Alice should work on her gross motor skills before tackling fine motor tasks – if she does not get enough practice on this, she will always find fine motor activities, especially writing, difficult

CASE STUDY 11

A child with dexterity problems

Zoë has difficulty holding and manipulating small objects, for example threading beads is a task she avoids. She seems to have an immature grasp and finds pencil and paper activities really difficult, changing hands frequently. When Zoë wants to go outside, although she attempts to do up buttons on her coat by herself, she always needs assistance to complete the task. When engaged in writing anything she holds the pencil so tightly and pushes so hard that she sometimes makes a hole in the paper.

Possible reasons for this behaviour

Zoë:
- may be suffering from a poorly integrated sensory system
- may have a weakness in the muscles associated with fine motor control
- is pressing very hard with the pencil as a means of gaining control over the movement

Strategies

- Arrange an assessment to help pinpoint Zoë's difficulties
- Try activities to strengthen fine motor control, such as: squeezing a koosh ball; using plastic tongs to pick up objects like paper, thread, feathers etc.; using scissors (especially designed for children with weak grips); using triangular pencils or pencil grips; using chalk or charcoal so that there is more friction when writing; using giant sized threading equipment; using bean bags or sponge balls for throwing and catching; using equipment and apparatus with varying textures; using sand trays for finger writing
- Make sure that the above is practised when Zoë is not tired and that it is carried out in short but regular bursts
- Use water and large household brushes for painting outdoors
- Zoë needs to have a wider experience of large movements: traditional games like hopscotch, throwing and catching large balls, throwing bean bags into a washing basket etc.

CASE STUDY 12

A child with poor visual tracking

Brian has great difficulty seeing the pictorial timetable which is displayed on the wall. Even when his key worker points to each picture in turn, Brian holds his head at a strange angle and appears not to be following her hand. When he is asked to copy his name from his name card, Brian strains to look at each letter in turn, even though he appears to be a bright and articulate child. He puts his finger on each letter but loses the sequence repeatedly. The resulting writing is completely illegible.

Possible reasons for this behaviour

Brian may:
- have visual problems in addition to his inability to track
- have sensory integration difficulties
- be demonstrating early signs of dyslexia

Strategies

- Develop Brian's gross motor skills and practise these on a daily basis, e.g. climbing, balancing, throwing, catching, riding tricycles and scooters. A programme should be drawn up so that each skill is practised regularly
- If Brian is required to copy anything he will continue to need it to be very close to him. This will become more important when he goes to school. Some schools expect children to copy from boards – this will be difficult for children with tracking problems
- Give Brian some sequencing practice. Begin by doing simple patterns, e.g. red, blue, red, blue, using equipment like beads, blocks etc. Progress to doing more complex patterns but build up slowly. When Brian is competent he would benefit from sequencing pictures, again, simply at first and then getting more and more complex
- Experiment with different coloured paper, although white paper with black text seems to be successful in most cases
- Experiment with different fonts
- Play games such as 'spot the difference'
- Play games such as letter or word searches – depending upon Brian's ability level
- Give Brian more time to carry out tasks involving letter or word recognition
- Give Brian a variety of strategies to help so that he can find the one that suits him to do activities independently

CASE STUDY 13

A child who cannot remember nursery rhymes and who presents with a generalised delay in the acquisition of speech

Tilly has been attending the pre-school for a year and a half and cannot recognise her name card. She is familiar with the routine and seems to enjoy all the activities on offer. She has immature play skills and her play is quite repetitive. Tilly tends to favour the home corner and playing with the dolls and buggy. Tilly uses mostly single words to communicate and still has trouble with naming the primary colours and joining in with songs and nursery rhymes. Staff have noticed that Tilly is not making progress with the curriculum.

Possible reasons for this behaviour

Tilly may have:
- a generalised learning difficulty or global developmental delay
- hearing problems

Strategies

- Refer Tilly to a paediatrician. This would help to eliminate any possible medical reason for her delay
- Provide a multisensory teaching method
- Use a visually strong method of teaching
- Teach Tilly at her own developmental level
- Give Tilly lots of repetition to consolidate learning
- Allow Tilly to experience new concepts with the aid of real objects
- Extend Tilly's vocabulary by beginning with encouraging her to name body parts, toys, clothes, people and pets, objects in her room, her house, her garden and then the wider world, the park, the pre-school etc. This will need to be extended to making choices between two items, rewarding her with her chosen item when she uses the correct word for it so that she can see the advantage of using language. This can be gradually further extended to using a noun and a verb to make her needs known
- Play memory and listening games. (See our previous book *Removing Barriers to Learning in the Early Years* (Glenn *et al.* 2005) for further ideas.)
- Tailor an individual education programme (IEP) focused on the above and share it with Tilly's parents/carers (see an example of Tilly's IEP in Appendix 2)
- Celebrate Tilly's successes and achievements

CASE STUDY 14

A child who does not recognise facial gestures

Aaron has poor eye contact and demonstrates some inappropriate behaviours like giggling when someone falls over and hurts themselves. When his key worker points to a picture of somebody smiling and asks Aaron to guess whether they are happy or sad, Aaron sometimes tries to guess but mostly ignores the question. When Aaron spoiled another child's drawing, his key worker pointed out that the child was crying. Aaron responded with laughter.

Possible reasons for this behaviour

Aaron may:
- genuinely not recognise the feelings of others or the facial gestures that go with them
- have difficulties associated with autistic spectrum disorder (ASD) and consequently have problems reading facial expressions

Strategies

- Observe Aaron's behaviour very closely
- Organise a paediatric assessment
- If Aaron is on the autistic continuum steps should be taken in order to meet his needs, e.g. he should be taught to read faces directly perhaps using simple line drawings. He may also need direct teaching of how to respond to people's feelings. This will help Aaron to become more accepted by his peers
- Help Aaron to develop some strategies to help himself, e.g. keeping a personal book about things such as faces and expressions appropriate to different situations, some polite responses to common questions, some common sayings etc. that people use (which can be misinterpreted by children with ASD). This can be added to whenever the necessity arises
- Encourage Aaron to talk about the pictures in books. He will need to be encouraged to talk about the characters in the stories and how they might be feeling

CASE STUDY 15

A child who appears distractible and presents with disruptive behaviours

Tom fidgets constantly when he is asked to sit down on a chair to do a task or to have a snack. He sometimes moves his chair back and forth making loud scraping noises or will bang it up and down on the spot. He appears not to have heard instructions even when sitting close to the adult at a table-top activity involving pencil and paper. Tom will on these occasions demonstrate disruptive behaviours and will sometimes just get up and walk away to play with something else.

Possible reasons for this behaviour

Tom:
- has sensory integration difficulties
- has balance problems
- may have difficulty filtering out unwanted sounds or movement or may be distracted by a visually busy environment
- may be aware that his more formal work is below the standard of peers and not as good as he would like it to be

Strategies

- Target areas for development with a sensory assessment
- Give Tom lots of opportunities to develop physical skills, especially gross motor skills. These can include walking along lines on the ground, playing hopscotch, balancing along very low beams with help at first and then independently, swinging, climbing, riding scooters and tricycles
- Sit Tom in a comfortable position, e.g.: his feet should touch the floor; the chair should be the correct size for him as should the height of the table; he should be shown where to place his non-writing hand so that he is properly balanced; he should be in an upright position; and he should be assisted to hold a pencil either manually or with the use of triangular grips
- Try a different environment, the acoustics can make a difference to children who are sensitive to noise. Similarly, too much visual stimulation may be a distraction and contribute to Tom's inability to concentrate. Consider placing tables used for more formal tasks in positions that are conducive to concentrating

CASE STUDY 16

A child who is inconsistent in levels of achievement and who gives up easily

Kayleigh appears to be a bright child and on certain days can recognise some words in her favourite story and can write her name completely independently. On these days she is co-operative and helpful. However, on other days, Kayleigh leaves tasks half done, seems to lose control of her pencil and generally seems to lose motivation and gives up on things almost straight away.

Possible reasons for this behaviour

Kayleigh:
- may be easily tired and on those occasions gives up quickly
- may have sensory integration difficulties
- may have failed at an earlier similar task and has made negative associations
- has a fluctuating degree of co-ordination difficulty and therefore presents with inconsistencies

Strategies

- Plan the more arduous, formal tasks for the morning if tiredness seems a problem – a lot of children get tired in the afternoon
- Arrange a sensory assessment
- Do not add to any negative tension that Kayleigh may have built up about writing. She may be 'giving up' instead of continuing so that failure is avoided. It is important that practitioners are sensitive to these things and highlight Kayleigh's achievements. It is important not to persist when she appears tired and cannot concentrate. Try to finish the session on a positive note, e.g. as soon as Kayleigh has had a success
- Give Kayleigh ongoing opportunities to develop her physical skills

Case studies (Practice)

The following are some case studies about bad practice and some suggestions about what can help. We are all guilty of doing inappropriate things at one time or another.

17. A session on letter sounds
18. Story time
19. Writing your name
20. Recognising and writing letter sounds
21. Making a Mother's Day card
22. Reading to a small group

CASE STUDY 17

A session on letter sounds

The scene

Children are seated in a large semicircle with an adult at the front, a considerable distance from the children. She is holding a very small cardboard letter 'T'. Another adult seated away from the group has called the register (this took about ten minutes because one child answered to all the names called and others copied in due course). The adult with the cardboard letter addresses the group.

'What's this'? There is no response. The adult spots a child holding something. 'What's in your hand?' 'Lego', replies the child. 'You are not allowed to hold that piece of Lego when we're doing our sounds – give it to Aunty Sally.' The child resists and starts to cry. Aunty Sally goes to the child and says, 'You will have to go to the office with the Lego if you are not going to put it away.' The child starts to cry even more loudly. There follows a scene where the adult takes the very reluctant child to the office where there is ever louder crying.

The adult with the cardboard letter struggles to make herself heard and to become the focus of attention. All the children are glued to what is happening in the office. She ploughs on, 'What's this?' Again there is no response. Some children are rolling onto their backs. 'All right then, what do you do when you go home?' 'Play', a child's voice rings out. 'No'. The child looks puzzled. 'Watch CBeebies', another voice calls out. 'No'. Children are chatting among themselves now and some are prostrate on the floor pretending to be aeroplanes with arms outstretched, making the accompanying engine noises. A third adult goes around the group and starts to physically arrange children into sitting positions. 'All right then, who has got this at the beginning of their name?' 'Amit?' suggests one little girl at the front of the group. 'Good, it's at the end, isn't it?' No response from the little girl but she looks thoughtful and then says, 'Is my mummy coming soon?' The child with the Lego comes out of the office looking very blotchy, taking loud shuddering breaths. An adult nearby explains, 'She is a very bright girl and often gets upset like this.'

The adult with the cardboard letter asks a child to find someone's name on the board with this letter at the beginning. The child puts it directly onto the middle of one of the names. 'That's in the middle, isn't it?' The group are by now getting really restless, the semicircle has disappeared and the supervisor suggests that they should all go to the toilet and then choose something to play with.

This is the end of the lesson on the letter 'T'.

Some suggestions

- Choose a topic relevant to children's own experiences, use teddies, toast, *Tweenies, Teletubbies, Thomas the Tank Engine*
- Do not allow yourself to become distracted – ignore unimportant events
- Use giant sized letters
- Use real objects and allow the children to hold them
- Use feely sacks
- Make items out of playdough
- Trace sounds in sand trays with fingers
- Find stories, rhymes and songs about the sound
- Use large visual aids
- Go outside and hunt for things beginning with the sound
- Share the learning objectives with the children
- Keep it brief
- Avoid the use of confusing language and keep to the aim – if a child says something irrelevant, answer but go back to the main teaching point
- Review with the children – have they understood?
- Plan accordingly

CASE STUDY 18

Story time

The scene

Children have been instructed to tidy up. Some of the children do but about eight or nine are carrying on with their activity. The adult in charge attempts to shout over the bustle, 'If you don't hurry up we won't have time for the story.' The children carry on much as before. Some children begin to gather on the carpet expectantly. The adult in charge starts to chat to two teenage girls who are on work experience and occasionally raises her voice with 'Are you tidying things away?' The adult busies herself with some display work.

The two girls sit down on some large cushions. More children gather on the carpet. Some carry on playing. The adult starts to go around the room shooing the children onto the carpet and puts the stray toys away. The group are all on the carpet and are chatting and fidgeting, some girls have their arms around each other and are swaying to some imaginary music. The two work-experience girls sit and look at the children. This goes on for some minutes.

One of the girls gets up and goes out to the corridor and comes back with a book. She sits and opens it with a weary expression. The other girl shouts 'Quiet!' After a few more 'quiet's there is a semblance of calm. Without saying anything the girl presses a button on the tape recorder. A voice starts to tell a story. The girl with the book and the weary expression begins to turn the pages. The children make a valiant attempt to follow the story. When it is finished, the girl with the tape says, 'Get your coats and line up by the door.'

Story time is finished.

Some suggestions

- Choose staff and work-experience staff very carefully and give them a very clear brief – children deserve enthusiasm
- Make instructions very simple and clear
- Demonstrate behaviours expected
- Use prompts like rainsticks, visual reminders, symbols etc. to gain the children's attention. They get used to shouting and become de-sensitised to it
- Always have books, visual aids, resources, puppets etc. ready well before the session
- Discuss the book and picture on the cover and engage the children with it by asking questions such as 'What is the picture on the cover of this book?', 'What do you think it might be about?', 'I'm going to ask you some questions about the cat/mouse etc. so listen carefully', 'Try to listen to find out what the cat's name is'

- Use large picture books and stop at intervals so that children can see the pictures properly
- Use an expressive, varied tone of voice so that children can pick up meaning from this too
- Round off the story by asking the children to re-tell it if appropriate or to evaluate it

CASE STUDY 19

Writing your name

The scene

An adult is standing by the door to the hall and as the children are coming in from the toilet she says, 'Go and find your name and put it on the table.'

The children mill around and some find their name cards and take them to their tables. A large group are looking at the name cards (which are all pretty much identical in appearance) and are searching for their own. Eventually, most children find their card with the help of an adult who is standing nearby and who is pointing to the right one. Three children are left by the table and the adult says, 'Come on, you did it yesterday.' She also addresses the other children who are involved in a variety of activities. A small group are sitting with their name cards at a table with a pencil pot and some paper in front of them. The three children still finding their names are eventually helped by the adult who gives them the right one. They join the small group at the table.

A group of six children are sitting at the table with the pencil pot and paper and the adult instructs them to copy their name. She then goes to each child in turn and comments on their efforts. She says generally, 'Are you using the same hand as yesterday?' There is no response. Some of the children are having great difficulty because the lines on the paper are quite close together and their name cards are only about three or four centimetres in height.

Some children have not developed a pincer grip so the activity becomes very difficult and they make a rushed attempt in an effort to get finished so they can join the others playing. The adult notices this and writes the name herself while the child watches. She then invites the child to 'go over my writing'. The child scribbles over the writing and puts the pencil down and says, 'Play sand?' (this particular child has Down's syndrome).

Some suggestions

- When introducing name cards make selected ones stand out by using colour, pictures or other clues. The clues given should be differentiated to reflect the ability of the child, e.g. a child who cannot read will need picture clues
- When asking children to find their name card begin by limiting the choices. For example ask them to find their name from a choice of two or three if they find choosing from the whole group difficult
- Make name cards large at first
- If children have difficulty recognising their name they are probably not ready to start writing it
- Make sure that you have large triangular pencils and pencil grips
- Use sand trays to write names with fingers

- Make sure that children have had adequate practice at gross and then fine motor activities, e.g. balancing, climbing, riding tricycles and scooters, throwing, kicking, catching, threading etc.
- Encourage the children to trace over simple shapes drawn by an adult. Then use letter shapes, starting with very large print and gradually getting smaller
- Use dot-to-dot
- Use large paintbrushes outside at first to make giant shapes with water
- Use large pieces of paper for writing
- Use whiteboards so that children can erase and try again if they want
- Use very large writing at first and keep it close to the child
- Some children are not ready for fine motor activities like writing if they have not developed their gross motor skills. If you suspect that the child is not making as much progress as you would expect, practise skills such as running, climbing, balancing, skipping, hopping, throwing, catching, riding tricycles etc.
- Children in the pre-school have not necessarily chosen which hand they favour for fine motor activities – do not worry about this but monitor it. This may reflect an arrested development and/or the general level of development, but it may also be that the child is concentrating on other areas of physical development, e.g. they may have just discovered throwing and climbing
- Practise using tongs to pick small items up to develop hand muscles

CASE STUDY 20

Recognising and writing letter sounds

The scene

About 23 children aged three and four are sitting around tables in a classroom in a nursery. The adult in charge is holding a card with a letter 'g' on it and is showing it to the children. She says, 'What is this?', to which there is very little relevant response. Most of the children are looking at her but do not seem to have understood. She says, 'What is this sound?' One child shouts, 'George'. The adult says, 'We don't shout in the Nursery' and then adds, 'It's a "g",' (making the phonic sound). She then points out that the children have worksheets on their tables and says, 'Colour in your "g" and write a "g" under the picture.'

The children busy themselves with the task. There is no further input from the adult. When the children give their papers to her, she puts them into a box and directs them to the other activities which are being put out by other adults. Some of the papers just have some marks on them. Some are very well done with recognisable letters on them.

Some suggestions

- Children in this group will be at varying levels of ability so this worksheet activity is not suitable for everyone. Also, although parents seem keen on worksheets because they are tangible evidence of their child's performance, they have very little meaning for children in the early years as young children do not connect the letter shape with the symbol and sound. They learn best by 'doing', so make the activity meaningful to their lives and experiences, e.g. finding as many things as they can that begin with the letter 'g', sorting items into those that begin with 'g' and those that don't
- Engage the children's natural curiosity at the start of the activity, when their attention is focused on the adult, by showing them a small display of objects that begin with the letter 'g' (e.g. gloves, guitar, toy garage, goldfish, gate, goat, golf club/ball)
- Identifying sounds in isolation is an abstract activity and has very little meaning for children of this age. Instead use real objects starting with the letter 'g' and allow the children to hold them, make the sound out of different materials, e.g. playdough, and use sand trays, to trace the sound with fingers. Make the experience as real and meaningful to them as possible
- If a child makes a contribution like the one in the case study who shouted 'George', acknowledge this positively (you can always remind all the children at the end that shouting is not really what you want)

- Support children while they engage with the task, demonstrate what you want them to do and reinforce their learning through the activity or task
- Give them feedback on their efforts and use the results to inform further planning
- Make sure that children are ready for writing tasks by ensuring they have had enough practice at developing gross motor and fine motor skills

CASE STUDY 21

Making a Mother's Day card

The scene

One of the tables in the pre-school is covered in newspaper and there are pots containing glitter, glue, sticky paper, tissue paper and other craft materials. Other activities are set out in the room. The children are sitting on the carpet after taking their coats off and the register is about to be called. When this is over, the adult directs the children to the activities by saying, 'You can choose what you want to do now.' The children go off to their respective activities.

One adult goes to the table with the craft-making materials on it and takes a list out of her pocket. She begins calling children to her and asks them to sit down. When four children are seated she gives them each a pre-folded piece of card and says that they will all make a card for Mother's Day. She tells the children to write their names on the inside and goes to each in turn to make sure that they are doing it in the correct place. Three of the children cannot remember how to write their names and so the adult writes it in dots for the children to go over. One of the children sees the glitter and says, 'I want to play with that.' The adult takes the glitter and shows the children how to stick it to the card with glue. The children begin to do this and the glitter is soon everywhere. The adult is making a flower out of the paper and tissue paper and sticks this onto each child's card. When all four children have a completed card the adult calls four more children to do the same activity.

This is repeated over a number of days until all the children have made Mother's Day cards.

Some suggestions

- Registration or whole-group time is for sharing learning objectives and the sequence of the day with the children. A visual timetable could have been on show so that the children knew what activities were going to happen that day. Instead of sending them off to play/choose, the adult could have used the time to focus their play on a particular theme, the activities could have been planned with a particular learning objective in mind. The planning could have been in the Plan, Do and Review mode so that at the end of the session, children feed back about what they have been doing.
- The card-making task could have been depicted in the visual timetable
- If an activity has no meaning for children is there a valid reason for doing it? So Mother's Day should have been explained to the children before the activity started
- The children should have been shown an example of a card – made by a child – so that they had a better idea about what was expected
- Demonstrate what you want the children to do in making the card

- Don't lose valuable teaching opportunities in this activity. These include: folding paper independently, making own marks on paper, opportunities for motor co-ordination by cutting, folding, scrunching paper, drizzling glue, using tools, writing own name or beginning letter of name independently (whatever it looks like)
- If an activity requires children to write their name the name cards should be available so that children can copy if necessary. In this way, attention is not drawn to children who cannot do this independently and they also get more practice at name writing rather than having an adult do it for them
- Tracing paper and paper clips should be handy so that children can practise tracing their name before going on to copying. Also name cards should have a recognisable starting point in a different colour and other aids like directional arrows if necessary
- Children of pre-school age are obviously not adept at craft activities but this is not an excuse for the adult to do the work for them. How many of the children can recognise their own card by the time Mother's Day arrives? Support but do not do the work for them – this is a temptation but resist it, celebrate the child's achievement if they have done what you wanted

CASE STUDY 22

Reading to a small group

The scene

An adult is sitting on the carpet with a group of six children. She has a book called *The Big Hungry Bear* which was chosen by a child called Rachel. The adult begins to read the story while showing the pictures as she does so. When there is a pause for the children to study the illustrations, Rachel says, 'I can read that book.' The adult responds, 'Can you – that's very good,' and continues to read the story. When there is another pause Rachel says, 'I know what's going to happen.' The adult ignores this and continues. When the adult gets almost to the end of the book Rachel interrupts with, 'The mouse cuts the strawberry in half and shares it.' The adult says, 'You spoiled it for the others, Rachel.' She then reads the end of the story and shows the pictures to the group. She asks the children if they would like another story and allows one of them to choose another book. 'I've got that one at home,' says Rachel and moves away from the group to play with something else.

Some suggestions

- Be aware of potentially able children in your setting – when Rachel said that she could read the book, it would have been a good opportunity to explore further. If opportunities like these are missed, it may send a message to children that it is often better to keep quiet because that is what adults seem to want
- It may have been better to suggest to Rachel that you would really like to hear her read the story to the group if she wants to do so. Or perhaps, find time to read with Rachel on her own to really assess what her reading abilities are (see 'Checklist for reading' in Appendix 1). It is important to differentiate between children who can genuinely read and those who are good at memorising text from familiar stories
- When Rachel announced the ending of the story she used the word 'half' and this could be a clue about her general level of ability. It is important to be aware of the language children use as this can be an indication of their level of ability
- If you highlight the fact that Rachel had 'spoiled' the story for the others this may be the unintentional main message the children (particularly Rachel) have been left with
- Rachel left the group at the end so the opportunity to explore her reading ability is lost for that session
- Be on the look out for able children and plan accordingly to extend their abilities and experiences
- Collect resources for able children – extensions of their interests, further reading materials, puzzles, games, interesting pictures and objects

- It is important to keep communication lines with parents/carers open so that they can participate in their child's education – some parents have very realistic ideas about what their children are capable of (some do not). Very able children can be quite exhausting for some parents and they may value some extra support with ideas and activities

SECTION 3

Activities

- Physical development
- Finger fun activities
- Speaking and listening
- Early phonics teaching
- Phonological awareness

Physical development

Physical development is vital for the later ability to develop reading and writing skills. It is even more important today when one considers the attraction of television and computer games over more traditional outdoor activities. Children are being placed in the supine position from babyhood, sat in baby chairs, car seats and then placed into baby walkers. Some children rarely exercise the muscles necessary for crawling (which develop as a result from being placed in the prone position).

Some children use a dummy for a prolonged period making speaking difficult.

Modern parenting and the changes to the way in which physical education is viewed may be having an effect upon the development of children and consequently upon their ability to learn skills like reading and, in particular, writing. Health visitors and pre-school practitioners are seeing an increasing number of children with immature gross and fine motor skills. Practitioners in the Foundation Stage have an important role in addressing this need especially since some parents are reluctant to allow their children much independent outdoor freedom.

Opposite is a collection of activities practitioners may like to consider when planning to develop the wide range of pre-reading and pre-writing skills. For some children, these activities should be practised on a daily basis during their Foundation Stage and for some, even after this.

Activities to promote motor co-ordination skills

- Walking along a line drawn on the ground, straight lines, wobbly lines, circles and spirals
- Balancing along low beams or on tree trunks on the ground
- Negotiating steps up and down (down can prove very difficult for some children)
- Jumping from low objects
- Hopping, skipping, hopscotch
- Dancing to music or to a rhythm
- Crawling in and out of tunnels, around apparatus
- Climbing
- Swinging
- Using scooters and tricycles

- Throwing and catching bean bags and then balls (sponge) of varying sizes
- Kicking
- Pushing
- Making large movements with arms – crossing the midline of the body, e.g. using large brushes to make giant shapes
- Running along flat ground, up and down slopes
- Using hoops
- Using bean bags for throwing, balancing, catching
- Rolling
- Using large saucers for spinning
- Stacking large bricks
- Threading large beads
- Threading smaller items
- Painting with hands, feet, fingers
- Making shapes in sand with fingers
- Doing puzzles, posting shapes
- Using peg boards
- Using tools like brushes, spades, knives, forks, tongs, scissors

Finger fun activities

The finger fun activities are important for developing the fine motor co-ordination skills needed for writing. Children need to develop the muscles in their fingers and hands in order to develop the pincer grip needed to hold pencils and pens. They also need to practise a range of activities in order to develop the control required for the fine movements associated with writing, cutting and threading. The frequent practice of these activities will help to consolidate children's growing abilities with fine motor skills

Finger fun activities to develop pre-writing skills

Activity	Materials
Sorting	Beads, macaroni, rice buttons, coins, peas, playing cards, sticks
Threading	Beads, macaroni, buttons, lengths of straws
Lacing	Laces through peg board, dot pictures
Matching	Shapes, sizes, patterns, colours etc. of any chosen material/objects
Peg design	Copy solitaire pegs/patterns in peg board
Stretching	Rubber bands or elastic around pin board, copy shapes or make designs
Cutting	Scissor activities – paper, playdough, fabric
Weaving	Cloth, thread, cane, paper
Pouring	To and from containers in assorted shapes and sizes
Jigsaws	Card, wood, plastic, felt
Games	Draughts, solitaire, pick up sticks, counter games
Construction	Lego, multi-link
Printing	Potato, sponge
Pen/pencil	Tracing (over designs and around shapes), colouring, dot-to-dot
Pottery	Punch and coil pots
Music	Keyboard, or wind instruments such as recorder
Pinching	Clothes peg/bulldog clip, and attaching around edge of shoebox or similar (use tripod pinch grip)

Speaking and listening

The activities opposite are important for the development of listening and speaking skills. It is very easy for adults to assume that very young children can distinguish between subtle differences in sounds used in everyday speech, but for this children need practice. It is vital, therefore, to provide opportunities for children in the early years to practise listening, starting at first with everyday sounds such as a car engine, a bus engine, a tap running, a water fall etc. These games can be fun as well as promoting the very important skills of listening and attention.

Activities to promote speaking and listening skills

- Listening to everyday sounds and being able to distinguish between different sounds/being able to distinguish between similar sounds

- Playing a range of listening games: 'simple Simon', 'follow my leader', 'I went to the shops and . . .', hide and seek, feely bags

- Using large picture books for observation and discussion

- Stories – listening out for particular things

- Nursery rhymes, poems and songs with actions

- Dancing to music

- Arranging some individual time to talk closely to children – they need to hear correct language modelled and having some quality time with an adult really helps to build skills and confidence

- Using puppets

- Use signing and alternative methods of communication alongside speech if necessary

- Use visually strong methods of teaching

- Use a pictorial timetable of the day

(See *Removing Barriers to Learning in the Early Years* (Glenn *et al.* 2005) for more ideas on attention and listening skills development.)

Early phonics teaching

It is important to make sure that children have been through the above experiences before beginning more formal phonics teaching. There is widespread agreement that phonological awareness is critical to reading success but teaching sounds in isolation has no real meaning for young children. The practice of 'doing phonics' by colouring in the letter shape on a worksheet and identifying appropriate pictures etc. is not the best way to practise a skill which should involve 'sounds'; make sure that any work on phonics is accompanied by children repeatedly hearing and saying the relevant sound, associating it with relevant objects and eventually linking it to the appropriate letter shape.

Phonological awareness

Rhyme

The child can:
- hear and say words that rhyme when spoken
- sort picture cards into sets that rhyme
- pick up an object from a feely sack that rhymes with an object you hold up
- generate oral rhymes and carry on a sequence like jelly, telly
- finish a well-known rhyming poem, song, nursery rhyme
- rhyme words in well-known word families, e.g. cat, mat, sat, pat
- generate a rhyming word when you say 'peg' . . .
- hear and say words that start with the same sound
- think of a word with the same initial sound when given an example
- hear when they do not start with the same sound
- sort picture cards into sets that start with the same sounds
- follow a group instruction to fetch an object starting with the sound signified by the letter you are holding up
- draw pictures of things that start with the same sound and that rhyme with the letter you are holding up
- understand that words which start with the same sound generally have the same initial written letter
- use the correct initial letter (mostly) in their own invented spellings
- use the initial letter correctly to predict words when reading

Segmentation

The child can say and clap along to words such as:
- dol/phin (two syllables)
- tel/e/phone (three syllables)

SECTION 4

How adults can help children to learn to read

Introduction

Paired reading

A print-rich environment

Introduction

All the adults involved with preparing young children for reading and writing need to be aware of the importance of providing clear and consistent messages about literacy and numeracy.

The methods of teaching reading have been controversial topics for many years in the popular and educational press but there is no doubt that, while different children learn to read in different ways and there is no one method which suits all learners, access to a wide range of pre-reading skills is essential if children are going to become proficient readers during their primary-school years. Unless exposed to regular and interesting print, children may not become acclimatised to the daily need for reading and writing which will make for successful learning.

Some parents are overly anxious that their children are given proper reading and writing 'lessons' and will need reassurance from the staff of the early years setting that a much broader range of activities needs to be provided so that children are truly ready to undertake the formalities of letter recognition and formation. Other families, on the other hand, appear to take a more laid-back approach to learning and resist any efforts to support their children in developing pre-reading and pre-writing skills, preferring to leave teaching entirely to the primary schools.

Parents can read to their children from a very early age – this is an enjoyable way of spending time with their child. Sharing books should always be a positive activity for all concerned. It is a chance to cuddle up on the sofa or in bed and this experience will help the child to associate reading with 'feeling good'.

Not all parents understand the importance of this activity, however, and some may lack confidence in 'doing it right'. Early years settings can do a lot to remedy this situation by inviting parents and carers to share in story time and watch an enthusiastic practitioner tell children a story and read through a book. This is an opportunity to model good expression, use different voices, make best use of the pictures etc. You could also give parents a 'help sheet' (see below) and allow them to borrow books – or encourage them to join the local library. Holding a 'bring and buy' sale is a good way of circulating books (and comics). (See Appendix 3 for ideas on running a parent workshop.)

Sharing books and stories

- Be comfortable, warm, relaxed

- Choose colourful books that are not too long – better still, let the child choose

- Spend time talking about the cover, the title of the book and who wrote it. Some books have no words – this is so that you can make your own story to fit the pictures

- When you read the text, use a finger to point to each word as you say it. This shows that you are moving from left to right across the page and that the words are important (but don't read in a stilted, word-by-word way!)

- Try to use expression in your voice: sound angry and fierce when the giant shouts, whisper when the character is scared

- Involve the child as much as possible; let them turn the pages, ask them what they think will happen next, what is their favourite page/picture. Ask the child to show you the front cover, the back cover, the picture on a page, a word, a particular letter, a full stop etc. – as appropriate to their stage of development

As children become familiar with words and begin the reading process for themselves, many parents and other adults may be hesitant to begin the more formal aspects of reading 'in case they get it wrong'. Paired reading is a tried and tested method of supporting readers of all ages.

Paired reading

Paired reading is a good way for adults and children to enjoy books together and also to help the children to read. It works really well with most children, and their reading gets a lot better. Most children really like it – it helps them to want to read more.

Books

Your child should choose the book, either from home, nursery/school or from a library. Children learn to read better from books they like. Don't worry if it seems too hard. Your child will soon get used to picking books that are the right level.

Time

Try very hard to do some paired reading nearly every day. You only need to do five minutes each day, if you want. Don't do more than ten minutes unless you really want to carry on. Any child can be taught how to do this.

Place

Try to find a place that's quiet. Children can't read when it's noisy or when there's a lot going on. Get away from the TV or turn it off.

Try to find a place that's comfy and sit so that you can look at the book together. Encourage the child to hold the book.

Get close, reading together can be very warm and snug.

How to do it

First of all look at all the pictures and talk about the pictures, asking questions and observing detail. This will engage the child in a stress-free way and 'cue' them into what is happening in the book, who it is about, what words they can expect to see on the pages. For example, if they see a picture of a boy on a skateboard and they comment on this, they are well prepared to read the word 'skateboard' even though they may never have seen it written down before.

Following this, paired reading has two steps: reading together and reading alone.

Reading together

You and your child both read the words out loud together. (It can often be a matter of the child repeating the word after you.) You must not go too fast.

In the early stages you could focus on one particular word in the story, e.g. 'pig' in *The Three Little Pigs*. Every time your child sees the word pig they can read it with you or they can give your hand a squeeze or a knock if they want to read it themselves.

Make sure the child looks at the words. It can help if one of you points to the word you are both reading with a finger. You can do the pointing together.

Reading alone

When you are reading together and your child feels confident enough they might want to read a bit of the story alone. You should agree on how the child will communicate this to you. This could be a knock, a sign or a squeeze. (You don't want your child to have to say 'Be quiet' or they will lose track of the reading.) When they make the sign, you become quiet straight away and allow them to take over the reading.

When your child struggles for more than five seconds, or gets a word wrong, you immediately read the right word aloud for them. Make sure they say the word correctly before continuing on. Then you both go on reading out loud together, until your child feels confident enough to read alone, and asks you to stop reading.

Ways of helping

With paired reading the hardest things to get used to are:
- When your child gets a word wrong, just tell them what the word says. Then your child says it after you. Don't make the child struggle and struggle, or say 'break it up' or 'sound it out' or 'you knew this word on the last page'
- When your child gets the word right, smile and show you are pleased and say 'good'. Don't nag or worry about the words the child gets wrong

Talk

Show interest in the book your child has chosen. Talk about the pictures. Talk about what's in the book as your child goes through it. It's best if you talk at the end of a page or section, or they might lose track of the story. Ask what they think might happen next. Listen to your child and don't do all the talking.

If you want to you can read the whole story again at the end of the session (together or the child can try it alone). Re-reading familiar books is a good way for the child to gain confidence and to practise using expression in their reading.

A print-rich environment

The early years setting should be a print-rich environment where children are surrounded by all sorts of words used for all sorts of reasons. For example:
- Displays – labelled nature table, photos of children and staff with names and captions

- Weather chart
- Calendar
- Word banks
- Letter–sound reminders
- Alphabet frieze
- Labels on cupboards and drawers
- Children's names on coat pegs, lunch boxes and work trays

Staff should be observed reading and writing notes and memos, writing on a messages board, writing notes for parents – and occasionally asking 'How do you spell . . .?' Talk to the children about what you are reading at home, 'I have just finished a lovely story about . . . It was sad at the end . . .' Let them see you reading letters, official reports and planning sheets.

A writing corner, post office and café can all provide opportunities for children to write 'in role', and practise their developing skills in a stress-free way. By emphasising different aspects of modern living the children will be given opportunities to practise a range of reading and writing activities with a purpose. Travel agencies in the high street will be quite happy to donate out-of-date holiday brochures which the children can look at and talk about; menus from pizza and other take-away establishments can make a suitable basis for a play restaurant to encourage the children to play at serving tables and writing down orders.

Remember that there is also a print-rich environment out in the street and shopping centres. Encourage parents and carers to point out to children:
- Street names ('Look, this is Saddle Street, it starts with an "s" – the same as your name Sam.')
- Bus stops
- Billboards
- Shop signs and names
- Notices in railway stations, tube stations and airports
- Street signs (STOP, LOOK RIGHT, LOOK LEFT)

The home also has the potential to emphasise the importance of print, so encourage parents to also be seen as readers and writers, and to make use of whatever they have to hand – newspapers, comics, catalogues, manuals as well as books. Some early years settings organise visits to the local library to show parents how to join and how to find appropriate books – and to assure them that there is no charge.

(When involving parents and carers in their children's reading, be sensitive to their own literacy skills. Many adults manage to get by with only a minimal amount of literacy skill and can be embarrassed if this is brought to light. In fact, their own children learning to read can be a great opportunity for them to brush up on their reading and writing skills if given appropriate support.)

APPENDIX 1

Checklists

Checklists to monitor progress in reading and writing

Checklists for identifying a child with DCD (dyspraxia)

Checklist to encourage reading and writing skills in the early years setting

Checklists to monitor progress in reading and writing

Checklist for reading

- Enjoys books and stories
- Handles books with care
- Pretends to read
- Knows that print conveys meaning
- Follows print with finger
- Recognises some individual sounds/words
- Shows an interest in reading
- Will talk about a book
- Can recognise individual words
- Uses pictures, context and phonic clues when reading
- Describes events in a story
- Predicts what will happen next
- Can read simple signs and notices
- Can read a range of material with some independence, fluency, accuracy and understanding
- Can read a range of texts fluently and accurately
- Can read independently using strategies appropriately to establish meaning
- In responding to fiction and non-fiction will show understanding of the main points and express preferences
- Will use knowledge of the alphabet to locate books and find information

Checklist for writing

- Hand used – left/right
- Has good pencil control
- Enjoys scribble writing
- Knows the difference between drawing and writing, numbers and letters
- Writes over teacher's example
- Copies under teacher's example
- Independent writing – is able to write without a model
- Uses the following to communicate meaning: pictures, isolated letters, isolated words, phrases
- Beginning to form letters correctly
- Can write some letters in response to letter name or sound
- Copies correctly from work card/board
- Knows all initial sounds
- Forms the initial sounds correctly
- Knows the alphabet
- Produces upper and lower case letters
- Uses them consistently
- Uses a word book
- Uses a simple dictionary
- Can produce lists
- Will attempt to spell common words
- Spells three-letter phonic words
- Will apply simple spelling patterns, e.g. feet, meet, street
- Can sequence events
- Understands that stories have a beginning, middle and an end
- Uses complete sentences
- Has started to use full stops
- Is often able to write in an organised, imaginative and clear manner
- Shows awareness of different forms of writing and different audiences
- Chooses a variety of words to create interest
- Usage of full stops, capital letters and question marks is accurate
- Handwriting is joined and legible

Checklists for identifying a child with DCD (developmental co-ordination disorder – dyspraxia)

The key signs and symptoms listed below should be used with caution – some may be applicable to pre-school children and others further down the list may apply to older children.

Gross motor

- Late motor milestones, e.g. sitting, crawling, walking and talking – child may not have crawled at all

- Hypotonic – child is often unstable around their joints, especially at hips, shoulders; a baby may show head lag

- Balance problems – child may be unreasonably afraid or conversely unaware of danger, child may be unstable if not sat properly in a chair with feet on the floor, may be easily knocked off balance and take a relatively long time to regain it

- Poorly integrated primitive reflexes – child may retain early baby reflexes, e.g. asymmetrical tonic neck reflex – they may turn their head one way and the opposite arm may go out

- Poor bilateral integration – child may find it difficult to co-ordinate both sides of the body; this makes using a knife and fork or handwriting harder to do

Fine motor

- Immature grasp and poor dexterity – there may be difficulty holding and manipulating objects, e.g. doing up buttons, holding and using a pencil, using scissors; the grip may change as the child changes posture; they may hold a pencil very tightly and may drive a hole through the paper; they may lie across the table to gain balance and control over the body to do a fine motor task

- Poorly established dominance – child may not seem to be clearly right or left handed, may use whichever is nearer to reach

- Poor pencil control, drawing, writing problems – child may avoid writing tasks and have a poor grip, child often has insight and realises that his/her work is not as good as peers, may be inconsistent, may function better when less tired

Eye movements

- Poor visual tracking – child may find it difficult copying, may use finger to follow print, loses their place when reading and listening to a teacher or others at the same time

- Poor relocating – cannot look quickly and effectively from one object to another

- Poor hand–eye co-ordination – the focus from the hand to the eye may be poor as well as vice versa

Learning difficulties

- Reading – failure or lack of progress

- Writing – difficulties with presentation, organisation of content, poor letter formation, letter reversals, writing may vary in size and quality from the top of the page to the bottom, letters may go well above or below the line, and consistency of form, spacing of letters and words may vary

- Maths – child may have sequencing problems, difficulty with remembering times tables, difficulty with abstract concepts

Language and communication

- Communication difficulties – delayed acquisition of speech, may present with 'sloppy' speech, may become less distinct when tired, odd thought patterns and sentence structure and difficulty organising content

- Poor receptive language – child may not understand language even though they have good expressive language, may talk a lot but out of context, may use complex but irrelevant vocabulary, may appear not to understand instructions or appear to be rude or sullen

- Social use of language – child may have difficulty understanding rules of a game, may find it harder to make and sustain friendships, may have difficulty noticing or interpreting facial gestures

Behaviour and emotion

- Distractible – child may be distractible due to inability to balance, inability to filter out unwanted noise, movement or visual stimuli

- Low self-esteem – child may be bullied by peers and adults who do not understand why they cannot or will not do things that are asked of them

- Frustration – child may be frustrated because they are aware that their efforts are not as good as those of their peers. This may result in poor behaviour especially in the home (at pre-school/school they may be able to control their frustration because of an awareness of social norms)

- Variability – child will achieve task on one day but not on another, may be affected by tiredness, may work best in the mornings

- Tension – previous negative feelings about poor performance may cause child to be anxious about attempting a task, may give up easily

Checklist to encourage reading and writing skills in the early years setting

- Coat pegs clearly labelled

- Designated areas and equipment labelled (with words and pictures)

- Writing area always available

- Regular newsletters to be taken home

- Opportunities for practising fine motor skills, e.g. buttons, zips, threading and lacing toys, building bricks and construction toys, doll dressing, fuzzy felts

- Use of cutlery when appropriate

- Displaying books in an accessible and inviting manner

- Clock on display and reference made to the time

- Visual timetable on display

- Calendar of events on display

- Adults seen to be using writing for purpose, e.g. making notes, making lists, writing letters

- Adults speaking clearly to the children and each other

- Variety of writing tools always available

- Children encouraged to sharpen their own pencils

- Sewing and weaving activities

APPENDIX 2

Recording pack

SEN register

Observation sheet

Observation sheet example

IEP – front of file detail

IEP tracking sheet

IEP – blank

IEP – Lyndsay

IEP – Tilly

Meeting with parents/carers

Special Educational Needs Register

Pre-school:		SENCO:		
Date:				

Child's name	DoB	Stage	Key worker	Date added to register

OBSERVATION SHEET

NAME: DoB: DATE:

PRE-SCHOOL:

REASON FOR OBSERVATION:

TIME:	OBSERVATIONS: record the context of the behaviour (the activity going on, people present etc.), the possible trigger for the behaviour (what happened immediately before), the exact behaviour itself – just as it happened (what you saw, not what you think about it).	INITIALS

ACTION:

OBSERVATION SHEET

NAME: Sam Marshall	DoB: 24.06.2000	DATE: 20.05.04

PRE-SCHOOL: Lark Lane

REASON FOR OBSERVATION: High dependency on adults

TIME:	OBSERVATIONS: record the context of the behaviour (the activity going on, people present etc.), the possible trigger for the behaviour (what happened immediately before), the exact behaviour itself – just as it happened (what you saw, not what you think about it).	INITIALS
9.30	Sam arrives with Mum and she takes off his coat and hangs it up, helps him to change his shoes and leads him by the hand into nursery.	AG
10.45	Sam has been playing in the water without an apron on – he is soaking wet but doesn't say anything to anyone. At snack time, KL asks him if he wants to change his clothes and he says 'yes'. She takes him into the home corner to change his top. He stands and waits for her to take off his top. KL hands him a clean T-shirt and says 'Put this on'. Sam takes some time getting it over his head – and ends up with it on back-to-front. KL takes it off again and puts it on the right way round.	AG
11.00	Most children put on a jacket to go outside but Sam does not bother. He asks KL to help him change his shoes. She is helping Katy and suggests Sam tries himself – he sits and waits for her to come.	AG
Action	Speak to Sam's mum about encouraging him to do things by himself. At nursery, set him one new task every week to complete by himself – changing his shoes, putting on his coat, tidying away the Lego etc. and praise him for his efforts. Start a star chart for this. Put Sam in charge of the fruit plate at snack time – handing round pieces of fruit to everyone in the group. Praise him for helping out. Review in 3 weeks' time.	

INDIVIDUAL EDUCATION PLAN – FRONT OF FILE DETAIL

NAME:	**DoB:**	**PRE-SCHOOL:**
ADMISSION DATE:	**ACTION/ACTION PLUS:**	
DATE:		

AREA(S) FOR DEVELOPEMENT:

LEARNING	BEHAVIOUR/ EMOTIONAL	PHYSICAL/ SENSORY

Detail:

SUPPORT DETAILS – INVOLVEMENT OF OUTSIDE AGENCIES:

PASTORAL CARE/MEDICAL REQUIREMENTS:

SPECIALIST PROGRAMMES/RESOURCES REQUIRED:

PARENTAL SUPPORT/INVOLVEMENT:

MONITORING AND REVIEW ARRANGEMENTS/FREQUENCY OF MEETINGS:

INDIVIDUAL EDUCATION PLAN – TRACKING SHEET

NAME:	DoB:	DATE:
KEY WORKER:		PRE-SCHOOL:

DATE:	TARGET: (1, 2, OR 3)	COMMENTS:	DATE ACHIEVED:

INDIVIDUAL EDUCATION PLAN

NAME: DoB: PRE-SCHOOL:

PLAN NO: ACTION/ACTION PLUS DATE:

AREA(S) FOR DEVELOPMENT:

TARGETS	STRATEGIES, RESOURCES, CONTRIBUTIONS
1	
2	
3	

TO BE ACHIEVED BY: REVIEW DATE:
SIGNATURES: SENCO: PARENTS/GUARDIANS:

REVIEW

1	
2	
3	

FUTURE ACTION

SIGNATURES: SENCO: PARENTS/GUARDIANS:

INDIVIDUAL EDUCATION PLAN

NAME: Lyndsay   **DoB:**   **PRE-SCHOOL:**

PLAN NO: **ACTION/ACTION PLUS DATE:**

AREA(S) FOR DEVELOPMENT: Attention and listening during story session

TARGETS	STRATEGIES, RESOURCES, CONTRIBUTIONS
1 Lyndsay will be able to sit on her own cushion next to an adult for the duration of one song in a singing session.	Lyndsay's key worker will sit alongside her and help her to join in with the actions by modelling. Use rewards when appropriate.
2 Lyndsay will be able to sit on her own cushion for a small-group, short story session.	Lyndsay's key worker will sit alongside her with a personal copy of the story book. Allow Lyndsay to hold the puppet in the story. Point out key things in the pictures. Gradually increase the number of children in the group.
3	

TO BE ACHIEVED BY: **REVIEW DATE:**
SIGNATURES: SENCO: **PARENTS/GUARDIANS:**

REVIEW
1
2
3

FUTURE ACTION

SIGNATURES: SENCO: **PARENTS/GUARDIANS:**

INDIVIDUAL EDUCATION PLAN

NAME: Tilly   **DoB:**   **PRE-SCHOOL:**

PLAN NO: **ACTION/ACTION PLUS DATE:**

AREA(S) FOR DEVELOPMENT: Learning delay

TARGETS	STRATEGIES, RESOURCES, CONTRIBUTIONS
1 Tilly will be able to name the body parts – head, neck, arms, hands, fingers, legs, feet – upon request.	Tilly will have one-to-one assistance for five minutes every day and her key worker will use a range of games/pictures/toys/rhymes/songs. Key worker to assess Tilly's progress weekly and then extend if appropriate.
2 Tilly will be able to begin to put a noun and a verb together to make her personal needs known.	Tilly will be able to make her needs known, e.g. 'go toilet', 'play buggy' after modelling from adults. Tilly will be offered choices whenever appropriate, e.g. at snack times, 'Do you want juice or milk?' Adults should model the correct responses, e.g. 'want juice'.
3 Tilly will be able to recognise her name card from a choice of two.	Tilly's name card will have a picture of her favourite toy on it. The first letter of her name will be written in a different colour.

TO BE ACHIEVED BY: **REVIEW DATE:**

SIGNATURES: SENCO: **PARENTS/GUARDIANS:**

REVIEW

1

2

3

FUTURE ACTION

SIGNATURES: SENCO: **PARENTS/GUARDIANS:**

MEETING WITH PARENTS/CARERS

Pre-school: **Date:**

Name of child:

Key worker:

Parent/carer:

Points discussed

Action

Signatures: Parent/carer: Key worker:

APPENDIX 3

The parent workshop

What is a parent workshop?

A typical workshop programme

What is a parent workshop?

Pre-schools may find it useful to set aside an afternoon, two or three times a year, to run a workshop event for parents, grandparents and carers to highlight the pre-literacy skills that all children will need in order to cope with the formal learning that they will receive when they enter mainstream school.

Most early years settings organise open afternoons, but a literacy-based workshop can be much more structured. It could include a short introductory talk by the early years manager, possibly a chance to meet one of the local education authority (LEA) representatives who visit pre-schools, and a demonstration of the sort of games and activities that are on offer in the setting, plus a chance for the adults to do some hands-on practical 'play', such as making and playing with playdough. (An activity such as this can be a very useful way for talking parents through the difference between upper and lower case letters, while reinforcing the need for left-to-right writing and the need for encouraging children to practise manual dexterity.) A checklist such as the one shown on p.86 might also be provided for parents/carers to take away with them. Many early years settings have developed excellent brochures describing in detail how their setting operates, but in many cases parents forget to refer to these once the children have started attending. Regular workshops will help to keep the families up-to-date on what sort of skills their children need and give them an opportunity to ask questions and gain insight into their child's development.

Tips for a successful workshop:

- Have a suggestions book open in the foyer
- Book swapping boxes
- Toy swaps
- Clothes swaps
- Diary of forthcoming events
- Birthday book
- Photo board of outings/events
- Hold a raffle

A typical workshop programme

1. Tea and coffee served round the table
2. A short introductory talk by the early years manager including introductions to other members of staff and, if possible, a representative from the LEA
3. An outline of the daily activities on offer in the setting – sand, water, playdough, construction toys, painting and drawing – and their place as essentials for preparation for reading and writing
4. A demonstration of letter formation and discussion of upper/lower case letters (with a handout of an alphabet with directional flow indicated for the parents to take away with them)
5. Three or four activities for the adults to choose from. These could be: making playdough to take home; threading toys, or following patterns of colour and shape with multi-link cubes; making a simple marble run; playing picture dominoes/arranging sequence cards; or playing visual discrimination games such as 'Guess who?'
6. Having a range of books and leaflets for the parents/carers to look at, and leaving enough time during the programme for questions and answers

Tips for a successful workshop programme:

- Create a welcoming environment
- Attractive visual aids
- Display resources
- A friendly face to meet and greet
- Name stickers
- Simple feedback form

Checklist of suggestions for parents/carers to encourage pre-reading and pre-writing skills

- Child's name on their bedroom door

- Labels in the house, such as fridge, washing machine, bathroom, breakfast cereals, video etc.

- Calendar with appointments written in

- Simple weather chart

- Analogue clock with clear numbers

- Car games to play, e.g. looking for the first letter of the child's name on number plates, looking for the numbers 0 to 9 on number plates, counting the number of Eddie Stobart lorries on long journeys

- Looking at shop names for the letters in the child's own name, making shopping lists using cut-outs from packets and choosing their own yoghurts etc.

- Helping to write birthday cards and postcards

- Playing 'I spy'

- Allowing time for the children to try and dress themselves to encourage sequencing and manual dexterity

- Getting hearing and eyesight checked if there is any concern about the child's progress

- Speaking clearly and using the correct name for objects

REFERENCES

de Bono, E. (1992) *Teach Your Child How to Think*. London: Penguin.

Glenn, A., Cousins, J. and Helps, A. (2005) *Removing Barriers to Learning in the Early Years*. London: David Fulton Publishers.

Weitzman, E. (1992) *Learning, Language and Loving It*. Toronto: Hanen Centre.

FURTHER READING

Burnett, A. and Wylie, J. (2002) *Soundaround*. London: David Fulton Publishers.

Call, N. and Featherstone, S. (2003) *The Thinking Child: Brain-based Learning for the Foundation Stage*. London: Network Educational Press.

Call, N. and Featherstone, S. (2003) *The Thinking Child Resource Book*. London: Network Educational Press.

Clipson-Boyles, S. (2001) *Supporting Language and Literacy 3–8*. London: David Fulton Publishers.

Costello, P. J. M. (2000) *Thinking Skills and Early Childhood Education*. London: David Fulton Publishers.

Drifte, C. (2003) *Literacy Play for the Early Years: Learning through fiction*. London: David Fulton Publishers.

Fisher, R. (1990) *Teaching Children to Think*. Oxford: Blackwell.

Godwin, D. and Perkins, M. (2002) *Teaching Language and Literacy in the Early Years*. London: David Fulton Publishers.

Griffiths, F. (ed.) (2002) *Communication Counts: Speech and language difficulties in the early years*. London: David Fulton Publishers.

Koshy, V. (2002) *Teaching Gifted Children 4–7*. London: David Fulton Publishers.

Medway Council (2003) *Guidance on Gifted and Talented (Very Able) Children in the Foundation Stage*. Medway: Medway Council.

Palmer, S. and Bayley, R. (2004) *Foundations of Literacy: A balanced approach to language, listening and literacy skills in the early years*. Stafford: Network Educational Press.

Taylor, J. (2001) *Handwriting*. London: David Fulton Publishers.

Whitehead, M. (1999) *Supporting Language and Literacy Development in the Early Years*. Milton Keynes: Open University Press.

Whitehead, M. (2004) *Language and Literacy in the Early Years*. London: Sage.

USEFUL ADDRESSES

The British Association for Early Childhood Education
136 Cavell Street
London E1 2JA
Tel: 020 7539 5400
www.early-education.org.uk

The British Dyslexia Association
98 London Road
Reading RG1 5AU
Tel: 0118 966 2677
www.bda-dyslexia.org.uk

Learning and Teaching Scotland
Glasgow Office:
74 Victoria Crescent Road
Glasgow G12 9JN
Tel: 0141 337 5000
www.ltscotland.org.uk/earlyyears

The National Autistic Society
393 City Road
London EC1V 1NG
Tel: 020 7833 2299
www.nas.org.uk

National Literacy Trust
Swire House
59 Buckingham Gate
London SW1E 6AJ
Tel: 020 7828 2435
www.literacytrust.org.uk

OAASIS
Office for Advice, Assistance, Support and Information on Special Needs
Brock House
Grigg Lane
Brockenhurst
Hampshire SO42 7RE
Helpline: 0906 863 3201(calls charged at a per-minute rate)
www.oaasis.co.uk

PECS (Picture Exchange Communication System)
Pyramid Educational Consultants UK Ltd
Pavilion House
6 Old Steine
Brighton BN1 1EJ
Tel: 01273 609555
www.pecs.org.uk

Pre-school Learning Alliance
69 Kings Cross Road
London WC1X 9LL
Tel: 020 7833 0991
www.pre-school.org.uk